MY
FAVORITE
FUNNY
STORY

MY FAVORITE FUNNY STORY

By

BILLY GRAHAM

ALFRED HITCHCOCK

SAM LEVENSON

BARRY GOLDWATER

POPE JOHN XXIII

JACK PAAR

YOGI BERRA

JOHN LENNON

GROUCHO MARX

ROBERT KENNEDY

and many, many others

Compiled by Bill Adler

Illustrations by Al Kilgore

About COMICS

Camarillo, California

Original hardcover edition published by Four Winds Press, 1967.

Paperback edition published by About Comics, October 2020.

ISBN-13: 978-1-949996-26-5

Customized editions available

Direct all inquiries to questions@aboutcomics.com

CONTENTS

I am most grateful to my excellent research staff for their assistance in the preparation of this book. They are David Curtis, Elaine Crane, Catherine Johnston, Janice Van Raay. Together we had a delightful time working on this book.

INTRODUCTION

Many famous people are famous because they tell funny stories. This is the comedian's job. But funny stories are hardly the exclusive property of professional comics; rather, as this book hopes to show, many of the most hilarious anecdotes and jokes come from personalities who, although well-known, are not usually noted for their humor.

Entertainers are, of course, the group most productive of humorous stories. Entertaining people often involves amusing them, and entertainment people are generally the most likely to publicize their funny experiences. Thus, a great many of our stories are told by the great stars of films, television, and the stage, including such names as Douglas Fairbanks, Jr., Bette Davis, Richard Burton, Sam Levenson, Bob Hope, Jack Paar, Peter Lind Hayes, and Groucho Marx.

Another group whose public nature often requires or produces humorous stories are the politicians. Any speechmaker can tell you that nothing can break the ice with an audience as quickly as a laugh-provoking story or two. Moreover, many of the most illustrious politicos can vouch for the pointed story as a potent weapon in debate. Few have been more adept at this form of political argument than Lyndon Johnson, John F. Kennedy, Winston Churchill, and Adlai Stevenson, many of whose stories are included herein.

The sports world certainly contributes more than its fair share to mankind's general hilarity. Like entertainers and politicians, sports figures often distinguish themselves as much by their personalities as by their abilities, and "characters" like Leo "the Lip" Durocher, Joe Garagiola, and Yogi Berra are as beloved of the public as many in the entertainment world.

Nor is the world of the arts without a goodly number of great wits. Towering geniuses like Pablo Picasso, Frank Lloyd Wright, and Igor Stravinsky all have delightful senses of humor to match their creative gifts, and seem to enjoy using the former almost as much as the latter.

A final group, far too often overlooked in the search for humor, are the men of the cloth. Most people, even if they don't take religion seriously, believe that religion is serious business, and therefore often dismiss the possibility of a clergyman with a sense of humor. Yet men like Billy Graham, Bishop Fulton Sheen, and Cardinal Spellman, with their great wisdom, compassion, and humility, possess qualities which produce some of today's greatest and most enduring humor.

Most of the stories that follow are true; many, probably, are creatively embroidered; quite a few may be apocryphal; and some are, beyond doubt, pure fabrications. All, however, are some of the funniest stories by famous people that you will ever hear.

BILL ADLER
New York City

✦ ✦ ✦ ✦ ✦ ✦ THERE'S NO PEOPLE LIKE SHOW PEOPLE

Alfred Hitchcock receives an enormous amount of mail, and tells this story about one particular piece of correspondence.

"One man wrote to me after I had Janet Leigh murdered in a bathtub in the movie *Psycho* that his wife had been afraid to bathe or shower since seeing the film. He asked me for suggestions as to what he should do.

"I wrote back, 'Sir, have you considered sending your wife to the dry cleaner?'"

Oscar Levant recalls the time he was playing an especially brilliant passage from Gershwin's "Piano Concerto in F" during a college concert. Suddenly a telephone began ringing in a nearby office. Levant ignored the persistent ringing, but soon the audience began fidgeting. Finally, without interrupting his playing, Levant looked out at the audience and said, "If that's for me, tell them I'm busy."

Comedian Alan King recalls that once he was told after a command performance in London he would meet Queen Elizabeth. For two days he carefully practiced his greeting. "How do you do,

Your Majesty. How do you do, Your Majesty." Hour after hour, he intoned the phrase in anticipation of the meeting with the Queen.

The awaited night finally arrived and King was introduced to Her Majesty. "How do you do, Mr. King," she said.

"How do you do, Mrs. Queen," he answered.

☆

Tallulah Bankhead, noted for her husky voice, tells that Earl Wilson once asked her, "Are you ever taken for a man on the phone?"

Retorted Tallulah, "No, are you?"

☆

Sammy Davis, Jr., tells of the time he was teeing off on a golf course when his opponent asked him what his handicap was.

"Handicap?" shot back Davis. "Talk about handicap — I'm a one-eyed Negro Jew."

☆

Sam Levenson relates this story about the early experience of his family in America.

"My folks were immigrants," he said, "and they fell under the spell of the American legend that the streets of America were paved with gold. When Pop got here, though, he found out three things: (1) The streets were *not* paved with gold; (2) the streets were not even paved; (3) *he* was supposed to do the paving."

☆

George Jessel recounts the story about the devout Catholic girl who fell desperately in love with a Jewish boy. "Teach him the virtues of Catholicism," advised her mother. "Make a convert of him!"

"That's just what I'll do," said the girl, and began to work earnestly that very evening.

The Jewish lad proved an easy convert. He became more enthusiastic as the days passed. Suddenly, however, one day before the wedding, the bridegroom canceled all plans. "What happened?" cried the distracted mother.

"I oversold him," wept the girl. "Now he wants to be a priest!"

☆

The Beatles' John Lennon tells of the time the brash British group was performing before a lavishly dressed audience at a Royal Command variety performance.

Introducing one number, Lennon remarked, "Would people in the cheaper seats please clap their hands? The rest of you can rattle your jewelry."

☆

Dave Garroway tells about a Chicago merchant he knows who was called suddenly to a big business meeting in New York. It was scheduled to last four days, and he had to catch a plane at the airport within the hour. How was he to contact his wife who was on a shopping spree in the Loop? The merchant thought hard and came up with a terrific idea. He told his secretary to cancel all of his wife's charge accounts. She called up in a rage twelve minutes later.

☆

Jerry Lewis tells about the time he was at a Florida hotel, where one morning at seven o'clock a tip-hungry bellboy knocked on the door. "Telegram, sir," the bellboy announced.

"Oh, all right," mumbled Lewis. "Just slip it under the door."

"I can't," answered the bellhop. "It's on a tray."

Shelley Winters recalls how she refused to prepare for a radio interview by Tex McCrary and Jinx Falkenburg with even one rehearsal. However, instead of stumbling over the questions put to her, she fielded them with ease and grace. Asked to "list the five men who've been in the public eye since 1900 with whom you'd most like to spend an evening," her five choices were Einstein, Toscanini, General Hoyt Vandenberg, Winston Churchill, and Laurence Olivier. The next question was, "What would you talk to those men about?" She replied that she would discuss Einstein's latest formula with the father of relativity; Toscanini's interpretation of his favorite symphony with the great conductor; strategic versus tactical warfare with General Vandenberg; the difference between the British and American constitutions with Churchill.

"I wouldn't waste time talking with Olivier," she added. "I'd just ask him to come back after the others had left."

☆

Peter Ustinov tells this story about a matinee performance.

"Latecomers were still straggling in when a lady's voice from the audience began counting,

14

'One . . . two . . . three . . .' in a loud voice. The suspense got worse as the counting continued. The other actors and I began to forget our lines in our fascination with the disconcerting performance in the audience. 'Six . . . seven . . . eight . . .' There was complete confusion on stage.

"Finally," Ustinov continues, "the lady got to ten. She half rose in her seat, waved toward the back of the house, and chirped, 'Yoo-hoo, Penelope, here I am — in the tenth row!' "

☆

One of Danny Thomas's favorite stories concerns a wealthy old man who was strolling through the business district of his city one evening, and as he passed a pet store, he heard the strains of familiar music. It was, in fact, the great music of his Jewish faith, the *Kol Nidre.*

The man entered the pet store as though hypnotized by the music. To his astonishment he heard and saw that the music was coming from a parrot!

The man decided that he must have the bird, costly though it proved to be. He bought the parrot and took it home.

15

Every night after that he sat on his back porch rocking to and fro while the parrot chanted simple little Sabbath hymns. The man was so happy he could hardly wait for the high holidays. Finally Rosh Hashana arrived. He hurried to the tailor and had a prayer shawl and a little black hat made for his parrot, just like his own outfit.

On the day of Rosh Hashana they went to the synagogue. The old man went up the steps and the parrot followed close behind. At the front door the caretaker stopped him.

"Wait," he said. "Where are you taking the bird? This isn't the zoo."

"Don't be so smart," the man replied. "That bird can pray better than you, the cantor, the rabbi and I put together."

The caretaker's natural reaction was: "Put your money where your mouth is."

So they made a little wager, and while they were betting, other members of the congregation came up the steps. Soon they were all in the argument and all wanted to bet. Finally the old man's stake reached a total of $4,800.

He was overjoyed. "Wait till you hear that bird make you lose all that money. Okay, sweetheart, let's have a little chant."

The bird remained silent.

"Darling, we're waiting. Go ahead . . . make a little chant . . . something simple like this . . ." He hummed a few notes.

Nothing but silence from the bird. For half an hour he pleaded in vain; the bird would not even chirp. The crestfallen owner lost the entire $4,800.

The old man was irate and embarrassed. Grabbing the bird by the throat, he rushed home. He threw the bird on the floor and went into the kitchen where he took the largest butcher knife he had and started to sharpen it. The parrot heard him sharpening the knife and flew into the kitchen. He stared at the old man and finally asked, "What are you doing?"

"You got a tongue now? You're talking? Got your voice back? Wouldn't make one chant and cost me $4,800! I'm going to cut off your head."

"Wait, wait," cried the parrot. "Don't be such a fool! Wait for Yom Kippur — we'll get bigger odds!"

☆

Charlie Chaplin relates a story concerning a dinner given in Hollywood to celebrate his birthday. Chaplin himself provided entertainment all evening long by imitating famous people, children, his chauffeur, even his Japanese servant.

Finally he sang at the top of his voice an aria from an Italian opera, and did an outstanding job.

"Why, Charlie, I never knew you could sing so beautifully," one guest exclaimed.

"I can't sing at all," Chaplin replied. "I was only imitating Caruso."

☆

Hermione Gingold relates that when she and her husband were divorced, he was broke and she didn't ask for alimony. Now, however, he is rather well-off. Recently she met him at a party.

"Darling, what about alimony?" asked Hermione.

"My dear," replied her ex-husband, "I would never take money from a woman."

☆

One of Mike Wallace's favorite stories is about "the time that Mrs. Truman went to a Grange meeting in Independence, attended by farmers from nearby localities. She went with a friend whose husband was the chief speaker of that day.

"The topic was 'Conservation of the Soil' and the man was a forthright speaker with a clear, forceful voice. He ended by summarizing his points and then he pounded the stand in front of him as he said, 'Just remember — what you need is manure, manure — and more manure!'

"His wife was embarrassed and whispered to Bess Truman, 'Oh dear, I've been trying to get him to say fertilizer!' Mrs. Truman whispered back, 'I've been trying to get Harry to say manure!'"

☆

Jack Paar believes that TV interviewers rarely listen to the personalities they are interviewing, a habit that results in some hilarious and embarrassing moments. He cites this story about an interview with journalist Cornelius Vanderbilt, Jr., as an example.

"The announcer asked Vanderbilt about his most exciting experience.

"'It was during World War II,' the journalist said, 'and I was covering the fighting on the Russian front. One day I was captured by Russian troops. I was thrown into an armored car and driven wildly through the night to an unknown destination. When I was dragged out of the car I was stunned to see we were at the Kremlin. My captors hauled me into that forbidding bastion, down a long, gloomy corridor, and finally hurled me to the floor. Looking up I saw Stalin glowering down at me!'

"At this point Vanderbilt paused for breath in his harrowing story. 'I see,' said the nervous announcer. 'Do you have any hobbies?' "

☆

Peter Lind Hayes stopped one day to watch an impromptu open-air chess tournament in Washington Square. There he saw one frail old codger, so weatherbeaten he scarcely could move the chessmen. Yet he beat every opponent with such ridiculous ease that Hayes hardly could believe his eyes.

"Pop," he asked, "to what do you owe your amazing stamina and clarity of mind?"

"Sensible habits," said the victor. "Every day since I was fourteen I've imbibed two quarts of whiskey, used beer for a chaser, and made love to a different girl in the afternoon and evening."

"Amazing," marveled Hayes. "How old are you?"

"Going on twenty-two," was the reply.

Arthur Godfrey tells the one "about the two fellows at three o'clock in the morning, talking about the use of words and how people get them mixed up.

"One of them said, 'Let me show you the difference between three similar words — irritation, aggravation, and frustration. You watch me.'

"So he went over to the phone booth and put a dime in it. First he picked a number at random from the phone book. Then he dialed that number, and a sleepy voice answered, 'Hello?'

"He said, 'Is Winterbottom there?'

"The fellow at the other end said, 'What number do you want?'

"He said, 'Superior 1-2345.'

" 'No, you have the wrong number. There's nobody here by that name. Now, do you mind letting me get back to sleep?' And he hung up.

"The guy said, 'See? That's irritation. That's what you call irritation.'

"Twenty minutes later he went back to the phone and dialed the same number. This other guy answered the phone and said, 'Hello!'

" 'Is Winterbottom there?'

"The fellow said, 'Look, I told you there isn't anyone by that name here at this number. Now,

go to sleep, and let me go to sleep, you dumb jerk.'

"The guy hung up, and said to his friend, 'That's aggravation.'

"Then about half an hour later he dialed the same number again. This time the fellow answered the phone and said, 'HELLO!'

"The guy said, 'This is Winterbottom. Have there been any calls for me?' That's real frustration."

☆

French comedian Fernandel tells of the time he went to a new barber. Excited at having such a famous customer, the barber pranced about him and could hardly do enough. Finally he finished. He held a mirror in back of Fernandel's head and whispered, "Is that all right?"

Fernandel looked at him coldly. "Almost. Just a little longer in back, please."

☆

"For my first radio appearances," Jack Benny relates, "I was paid $350; for my first television show $10,000. The only similarity between those appearances was the amount of money the government let me keep."

Jack E. Leonard tells the one about the "two Indians, Falling Rocks and Crazy Horse, who were competing to determine who would be chief. Both went into the wilderness to hunt. Many moons later Crazy Horse returned with seven elk and five bear. Falling Rocks never returned. To this day, as you drive along the highway there are signs that say: 'Watch out for Falling Rocks.' "

☆

Walter Cronkite tells the story of the TV and radio networks spending millions to move their computers, cameras, equipment, and crews to New Hampshire to cover the primary. "Fewer than 10,000 people voted in that primary," he says, "and I think that hereafter it would be better for us simply to bring those 10,000 voters to New York, put them up for a few days, and save an awful lot of money."

☆

Jim Backus lived near a rich movie tycoon whose overindulged twelve-year-old son ran away from home. Relates Backus, the outraged father called over to him, "How do you like that? A twelve-year-old brat running away from his mother and father!"

"Take it easy," consoled Backus. "Your son is like many other youngsters, rebelling against authority. All twelve-year old kids at one time or another run away from home."

"What?" bellowed the tycoon. "In a Thunderbird?"

☆

Oil tycoon Paul Getty remembers being interviewed in London. "If you retired now," asked the reporter, "would you say your holdings would be worth a billion dollars?"

Getty paced up and down the room, mentally tallying his assets. "I suppose so," he answered. "But remember, a billion doesn't go as far as it used to."

☆

Jack Paar tells that once when he arrived in London, a British friend told him that on checking into the hotel he should ask the telephone operator to get Buckingham Palace and leave a message for the Queen to call him.

"She won't, of course," the friend said, "but you'll get great service at the hotel when the word gets around."

Johnny Carson enjoys telling how once on the TV show *Tonight*, the president of the American Heart Association came on and, flustered, launched his speech with his back to the camera. "Doctor, it's National *Heart* Month," Carson said gently, turning him around. "We have the wrong part of the anatomy."

☆

Television moderator John Daly recounts that he had to explain to a large audience that a slight problem had arisen in the show's format. "Ladies and gentlemen," announced Daly, "the guest of honor this evening needs no introduction — he didn't show up."

☆

Actor David Niven tells of a day with friends when a pretty red-haired woman came by and cried "David!" Niven instantly leaped to his feet, kissed her, and cried, "Darling!"

Suddenly he frowned and, turning to his companions, shielded the woman. "She's all mine," he declared. "I shan't share her with any of you." He led his delighted acquaintance a few steps off and chatted, kissing her hand again as she departed. After she had left, Niven's friends asked him why he had acted as if he wanted to abduct her.

"You'll have to forgive me," Niven apologized. "I couldn't remember who the devil she was and I couldn't take the chance."

☆

Jackie Gleason relates that the day after he had been awarded a Tony statuette, Broadway's equivalent of an Oscar, for his performance in *Take Me Along*, he telephoned his friend Toots Shor. "Well, Toots," said Jackie, "I finally got that wonderful thing I've been trying to get for so long."

"So I heard," Shor said.

"Now I'm trying to figure where I ought to put it in this house of mine," Gleason said.

"On the wall over your bar," Shor suggested.

"Are you out of your mind?" Gleason replied. "How can I put the Dodgers' old bench from Ebbets Field up on a wall?"

☆

Carol Channing reports that in her night-club act she sometimes invited the audience to ask her personal questions. One evening a man at a ring-

side table strode up and asked her, "Do you remember the most embarrassing moment you ever
had?"

"Yes, I do," Miss Channing answered. "Next
question?"

☆

Fernandel, the French comedian, tells of the
time a certain impresario came to see him. On
taking his leave, the impresario saw an open box
of cigars on the table, and said: "What wonderful
cigars! Would you allow me to take one or two to
smoke on my way home?"

"Certainly," answered Fernandel. Then, noticing that the impresario helped himself to at least a dozen, he added: "I'm very grateful to you for coming to see me from such a long distance."

David Niven tells that when he was mess officer for the Highland Light Infantry, he once purchased some high-grade caviar from a Russian ship. That night as a great treat he served it at general mess. To his surprise there was a great deal of complaining among the men. Finally he asked one old-timer what was wrong.

"Well," said the soldier, glaring at Niven, "the bloody blackberry jam tastes of fish."

Joey Bishop tells the one about "the golf hustler who had beaten everybody, and so finally three guys go to Africa and they actually train a gorilla to hit a golf ball. This gorilla hits a ball 430 yards. It's the easiest shot, and they import this gorilla from Africa and bring him over to play this hustler. The gorilla takes off and hits the ball 430 yards, and it lands four inches from the cup.

"Now they hand him the putter. He hits the ball with the putter 430 yards."

☆

Joan Crawford recalls that during a scene in *Possessed* she was to slap Van Heflin. Since they had had a few disagreements concerning the script, Van had a hunch that the slap would be one to remember. The scene was scheduled to be shot in the morning. However, due to lighting trouble, it was postponed until after lunch. During the lunch break Heflin called his wife who told him, "You just got a lovely bunch of flowers."

"Open the card and see who they're from," he said.

The card read, "Sorry to have hit you so hard, darling. . . . Joan."

The Beatles fondly recall the day Queen Elizabeth presented them with medals making them Members of the British Empire. When asked how the Queen had treated them, Paul McCartney replied, "She was like a mum to us."

☆

Art Linkletter likes to tell this story:
"During one broadcast of my TV show, *People Are Funny*, I announced to my studio audience that I was about to auction off something pretty rare — an opportunity to bash me in the face with a cream pie. The bidding was spirited; in no

time it got up to $200. At that point a woman quietly but firmly bid $225. She won promptly, wrote me out a check for the amount, took pie in hand and really let me have it — smack in the kisser.

"The next day her check bounced."

☆

Phil Silvers relates the story of a born financier in a rural hamlet in Indiana. His weekly pay check in the factory is $110 a week — but he never takes it home. He raffles it to fellow workers at a dollar a chance. In the past three years his earnings have averaged $700 a week — in cash.

☆

Arlene Francis tells of the day she encountered a movie celebrity wheeling her child in a carriage. "My, that's a beautiful baby," said Arlene.

"Thank you, but this is nothing at all," replied the star. "You ought to see him in our home movies."

☆

Martha Raye recalls playing a Catskill resort one summer and hearing a woman shout to her child who was recklessly climbing a tree:

"Joey, come down, do you hear? Come down or you'll break your legs. Joey, Momma's telling you! All right, Joey, but when you fall down and break both legs, don't come running to *me!*"

☆

Comedian Dick Gregory retells the story of the time he was in Biloxi, Mississippi.

"I walked into this restaurant and this white waitress came up to me and said, 'We don't serve colored people in here.'

" 'That's all right,' I said. 'I don't eat 'em. Bring me a whole fried chicken.' "

Movie star Anthony Quinn likes to tell this story about his young son, Frankie:

"We were in Miami where I was doing *Mr. Innocent* for Sam Spiegel and Columbia Pictures. I was leaving for location one morning, and Frankie didn't want me to go. Almost crying, he asked where I was going and I said, 'I'm going to work' and I started for the door. He ran after me, 'No, Papa, no. Stay with me!'

"I said 'But Frankie, I can't. I have to go to work. It's very important.'

"He jumped up and down. 'No, it's not important. Stay with me!' I tried to explain, patiently: 'But Frankie, if I don't go to work, I won't have any money to buy you toys.'

"He stood still, thinking, and then said, 'You better hurry — you might be late.' "

☆

John Barrymore recalled that when he scored his first hit on Broadway, he took an apartment in New York's Greenwich Village and spent his newly found wealth buying furnishings for it. He even built a garden on the roof. To accomplish this, tons of earth had to be hauled up.

Soon after the garden had been completed, it

belatedly came to the attention of the owner of the building.

"What have you done?" he wailed to the actor. "This roof cannot sustain such a weight. It will collapse!"

"Are you sure?" said Barrymore.

"Of course I'm sure. Now what are you going to do about it?"

"I'm going to move, of course!" retorted Barrymore. "You don't expect me to live in an unsafe building, do you?"

☆

Arthur Godfrey tells the story about "Pat and Mike, who just came over from the Auld Sod. They were stopping at a street corner in New York when the traffic light was red; then it turned very briefly to orange, and then it turned green. Pat looked at Mike and said, 'Faith, you know, they don't allow much time for the Protestants here, do they?' "

☆

Comedian Fernandel recalls the time he went to the dentist and had an aching tooth pulled. Several weeks later he got an envelope from the den-

tist. Inside, instead of a bill, was a neat sheaf of folding money with this note: "I've sold your tooth to one of your fans who is carrying it as a good-luck charm. From the proceeds I've deducted my professional fee and enclose the balance."

☆

Will Rogers used to tell a story about a friend who loved hunting, in spite of being a terrible marksman. One day he met the friend returning from an obviously fruitless day's shooting.

"Didn't you get anything?" asked Will.

"Not a durned thing," said the man. "I was so ashamed to face my wife again that I went to one of the local butchers who obligingly tied a live rabbit to a tree for me to take a shot at."

Seeing that he had no rabbit with him, Rogers asked, "What! Mean to tell me you even missed that?"

"Oh, I made a swell shot," said the fellow gloomily. "Hit the rope clean in the middle, and I haven't seen the rabbit since!"

☆

Gary Cooper used to recall that once, when he had finished making a certain picture for Samuel

Goldwyn, another producer, Hunt Stromberg, exercised the option which he held on Cooper's services. Goldwyn called the other producer and said, "It isn't that I mind your taking Cooper. But you could have been nicer about it. You could at least have called me up and said, 'Sam, I need Cooper right away, if it doesn't interfere with your plans.' Then, I'd have said, 'No.'"

☆

Jimmy Durante likes to tell the story about when he bet on a horse at Santa Anita and the nag lost by inches. "What that horse needed," bragged an ex-jockey, "was my riding."

"What he needed," countered Durante, "was my nose."

☆

Bing Crosby tells this favorite story when he meets an actor whose head is getting too big for his halo. It concerns the incident in a Broadway restaurant when a man approached his table and stuck out his hand. "Betcha don't remember me, pal," the man said. "Fourteen years ago I was entertainment chairman for our lodge and I risked my reputation hiring you for the show."

Bing, trying to be polite, grinned and said, "Sure, sure, mister — how could I forget?"

Thus encouraged, the stranger went on, "At that time," he said, "you were dead certain that someday you'd be a big radio and movie star."

Crosby nodded.

"So tell me," the man inquired, "what finally happened to you?"

Katharine Hepburn remembers that, when she was assigned to her first role at MGM opposite

Spencer Tracy, she was anxious about acting with a star who had already won two Oscars. But Katie wouldn't let anyone know it — particularly Mr. Tracy. Walking briskly onto the set with her mind made up that she'd get in the first word, she stared at Tracy for a moment, then warbled, "Oh, Mr. Tracy, I'm really afraid I'm too tall for you."

Spencer measured the upstart with a face devoid of all expression. Then he said calmly, "That's all right, dear. I'll soon cut you down to my size!"

☆

Jimmy Durante tells the story about the ball game being umpired by a runt of a fellow. An enormous player was at bat and an equally large catcher squatted behind him. The count was one and one. The little umpire, watching the pitch sizzle across a corner, yelled, "Two!"

"Two what?" snarled the catcher, mashing his mask into the umpire's face.

"Yeah, two what?" growled the batter, raising his bat.

The umpire looked from one brute to the other and said: "Too close to tell!"

Movie-producer Samuel Goldwyn recalls when he was looking for a young actress to play a role in a forthcoming picture.

"The girl who plays this part must have a wholesome, natural beauty," he told an assistant. "She must have the green of the trees in her eyes, the snow of the mountaintop in her teeth, the blush of the rose on her cheek."

"But Mr. Goldwyn," protested the assistant, "there's no such thing as a natural beauty in Hollywood."

"All right, then," said the producer, "we'll use a little make-up."

☆

Groucho Marx is fond of telling about the time, during the World War II days of rationing, when Oscar Levant flew into Los Angeles after a tough concert tour. In a touching display of friendship Groucho said, "Oscar, you look tired. Why don't you come to my house for dinner? I've got the most wonderful cook in town, I've saved a steak four inches thick, and we'll have a dessert that's out of this world."

Sighing gratefully, Levant asked, "What's your address?"

"Wouldn't you like to know?" replied Groucho — and strode away.

Lester Lanin tells of the golf nut whose fiancée was left waiting at the altar. She telephoned his golf club and was told he was on the eighteenth green. When he answered the phone, she sobbed hysterically about the utter humiliation of being left at the altar.

"But honey," he interrupted, "I told you over and over again — *only if it rains.*"

☆

Jack Paar is annoyed with the traffic problem in Manhattan, complaining that it sometimes takes fifteen minutes to go only a couple of blocks. He told about an exasperated fellow motorist who had been delayed for some time in one of those traffic jams. In desperation he rolled down his car window and hollered, "Let me through, will you! I've got important news for President Cleveland."

☆

Buddy Hackett remembers the time he and Arthur Godfrey were discussing a beatnik-type girl in the news who was making a plea for more police protection. "He asks what I think and I tell him, 'with this girl, there's nothing to think — her face is her chaperone.'"

43

Sam Levenson remembers the time his mother was walking down the street on the lower East Side of New York and stopped to look at some secondhand merchandise in a pushcart. She scrutinized a bent serving spoon.

"How much is it?" she inquired.

"A penny," answered the peddler.

"I don't know," she said, shaking her head doubtfully.

"Go ahead," urged the peddler, "make me an offer."

☆

Jack Benny tells about what a big kick he got out of it "when Waukegan, Illinois, my home town, named a new junior high school for me and I turned the first spadeful of earth for it. The other two junior high schools are named for Daniel Webster and Thomas Jefferson. I guess the three of us are about the same age."

☆

Jack Paar remembers that when he mentioned the merger of two companies on his TV show, the SEC immediately began to suggest that he was trying to manipulate the stock market.

"The only way I have ever manipulated the stock market was to sell," Paar confessed abashedly. "Whenever I sell a stock it immediately goes up."

☆

Tony Curtis says that when he and Zsa Zsa Gabor were filming scenes for *My Last Duchess* in Europe he observed her during a film break. Zsa Zsa put her diamond-studded hand into her diamond-studded pill box, and picked out one pill. She then turned to a stagehand and said, "Dollink, vood you be an angel and get me a glass of champagne."

Sam Levenson tells a story about a man who quarreled with his wife and moved to a hotel. All day he brooded, but by dinnertime he was hungry and sorry, so he called her.

"Hello, Sarah. What are you making for dinner?"

"Poison I'm making."

"So make one portion. I'm not coming home."

☆

Dick Gregory tells of an incident at a nightclub one night, when a woman stood up and said bluntly to Gregory, "I don't like you."

Responded Gregory with great nonchalance: "Christ had twelve disciples, and two of them welshed on Him, so what do you expect out of a room of two hundred and forty people?"

☆

The entertainer Nipsy Russell remembers that some years ago, when called upon to make a speech to the nine Negro boys and girls about to enter Little Rock High School surrounded by hostile troops and mobs, he stated at their pep rally the night before, "Children, I don't want you in your actions upon entering that white high school to in any way justify what white folks delight in saying about us — namely that we are savage, uncouth, barbarian. Don't go into that school carrying knives, razors, or guns. No. Be civilized. Go in there throwing atom bombs."

☆

Bob Hope recalls the way he and Jack Benny first met.

"Benny came up on a golf course and said, 'Need a caddy?' How can a man with his money be so cheap as to caddy for a few extra bucks? Walking up and saying, 'Need a caddy?' What made me so mad was that he didn't say it to me but to the guy I was caddying for."

☆

Danny Kaye likes to use this story to define *chutzpah,* a Yiddish word roughly meaning "effrontery":

"A classic example of *chutzpah* is a kid who murders his mother and father and then begs the court for leniency because he's an orphan."

☆

Jerry Lewis loves to recount the accomplishments of his son Gary, the leader of a very popular rock 'n' roll band. Now Jerry tells of how his five-year-old son, Ronnie, recently announced: "Dad, I've got my own musical combo. I know I can make it, and I just want you to know I'll make it on my own — I'm not going to trade on Gary's name at all."

☆

Milton Berle tells of introducing two of his friends, the Duke of Bedford and Max Asnas, owner of the Stage Delicatessen in New York City. Berle said: "The Duke of Bedford, meet the King of Salami."

☆

Douglas Fairbanks, Jr., says that soon after John F. Kennedy was inaugurated, he met the President in Washington. Kennedy asked him, "Do you still speak Spanish?"

Fairbanks nodded, then asked: "But, Mr. President, how did you know that I speak Spanish?"

JFK looked at the star mirthfully. "I know that because you and I went to the Berlitz class together. It's odd that I, the President of the United States, should remember — and you don't . . ."

Martha Raye tells of visiting an Army camp where a colonel was staging an inspection for her benefit. As they walked past the men, he barked: "Show that shoeshine!" "Let's see those finger-nails!" and all the usual inspection commands. In the silence after one recruit had been ordered, "Stick out your tongue!" Miss Raye's inimitable voice boomed out, "Now turn it over!"

☆

Bette Davis tells the story of how in January of 1963 her attorney called her at home on the West Coast to inform her of a rumor current in New York that she had just died. Miss Davis promptly answered, "With the newspaper strike on, I wouldn't consider it."

☆

Jerry Lewis tells about the battle-scarred heavyweight who refused a thousand-dollar bribe to "throw" a fight in the second round of a bout with a highly touted and overrated new-comer. The veteran's explanation was, "I never lasted till the second round yet, and I ain't gonna start now. The time I fought Joe Louis, I had him plenty worried, though," added the pug. "He thought he'd killed me!"

Zsa Zsa Gabor tells about receiving a mink coat from Generalissimo Rafael Trujillo of the Dominican Republic.

"He gave me a car," she explains, "and every time I drove with the top down, I got chilly. So naturally he did what any gentleman would do and offered me a coat."

☆

Henry Fonda, Hollywood celebrity and star of many Broadway plays, remembers being asked by Sandy Baron, "If you had to sum it up in one line — what would you say was the most important single thing a young actor has to know?"

Fonda replied: "How to become an *old* actor."

Phil Silvers relates that he once had a crush on Olivia de Havilland. She went out with him several times, but when he asked her to the Academy Award dinner, high point of the social season, she said, "I'll go with you — but you must promise to leave off those glasses. They make you look so silly."

Silvers promised and kept his word. He called for her that evening in white tie and tails, with a corsage of orchids — and a seeing-eye dog.

☆

Milton Berle tells how he once played Pittsburgh for a one-week stand. On Monday he chose a restaurant that looked good to him, and enjoyed everything except the bread. "I always eat whole wheat," he told the waitress, but she brought white. Tuesday, he reminded her about the whole wheat, but got white bread again. Wednesday she made the same mistake, and repeated it Thursday and Friday. Finally on Saturday when she took his order, Berle said casually, "Just for the heck of it, I think I'll take white bread today."

"That's funny," said the waitress. "Aren't you the party who always orders whole wheat?"

Bob Considine, the sports writer, tells about one fight in a second-rate arena that failed to satisfy the bloodthirsty spectators. The contestants circled each other warily, throwing practically no punches. After a long silence, a voice rang out from the back: "Hit him now, yah big bum. Yah got the wind wit' yah!"

☆

Art Carney tells a story about the clever brother who was always around when his pretty sister wanted to be alone with her boy friend. To get rid of him one afternoon, the boy friend suggested, "Why don't you go down the street, Willie, and count the men who are wearing red hats. I'll give you a quarter for every one that goes by." To the surprise of both sweethearts, Willie agreed to this suggestion. Fifteen minutes later, however, they heard his triumphant voice from below. "I don't know how you two are doing in there," he yelled, "but my ship is about to come in. Here comes the Shriners' parade!"

☆

Dinah Shore recalls this incident: "While we were in France entertaining the GI's, I was dining one night at mess with some officers. We were having steak, and it was very tough.

"Noticing my struggles, the colonel apologized. 'I know it's tough,' he said, 'but my orderly chased that cow ten miles before she would step on a mine!'"

☆

Humphrey Bogart told the story of the time he and Lauren Bacall were in the Stork Club when Harry Cohn, president of Columbia Pictures, walked over to their table and whispered a few words to Bogart. The actor turned to his wife and beamed: "The picture's a hit."

"What makes you so sure?" asked Miss Bacall.

"Because Mr. Cohn referred to it as 'our picture,'" Bogart explained. "If it were a flop, he'd have said 'your picture.'"

♦ ♦ ♦ ♦ POLITICS IS A FUNNY BUSINESS

In contemplating the issue of which direction — left or right — this generation will take, Illinois Senator Dirksen recalls "the days when circuit judges rode about on horseback. I am advised that down in Kentucky in those days when Abraham Lincoln was a member of the Illinois legislature, they had a judge who had a great fondness for corn liquor.

"One day," Dirksen continues, "when the judge was 'slightly mellow,' he went out to throw a saddle on his horse. A young lawyer watching the operation noticed that the judge had the pommel where the cantle should be. He said, 'Your Honor, you have your saddle on backward!'

"Then, with the kind of dignity that only the judiciary can assume, the judge said, 'How in the devil do you know in what direction I am going?'"

54

John F. Kennedy told this story about Richard M. Nixon during the 1960 Presidential campaign:

"I know, after fourteen years in the Congress with the Vice-President, that he was very sincere in his views about the use of profanity. But I am told that a prominent Republican said to him yesterday in Jacksonville, Florida, 'Mr. Vice-President, that was a damn fine speech.' And the Vice-President said, 'I appreciate the compliment but not the language.' And the Republican went on, 'Yes, sir, I liked it so much that I contributed a thousand dollars to your campaign.' And Mr. Nixon replied, 'The hell you say.'"

※

Allen Dulles, past director of the American Central Intelligence Agency, recalls the time he "was attending a diplomatic function which included Jozef Winiewicz, Ambassador of Poland.

"The flow of liquor thawed diplomatic frigidity. There was some singing, and someone suggested the ambassador sing a song.

" 'Yes, Mr. Ambassador,' Dulles urged, 'do sing for us. I understand you have an excellent voice.'

" 'You should know, Mr. Dulles,' said Winiewicz. 'You have enough recordings of it.' "

Vice-President Hubert Humphrey recalls that after his nomination as Democratic Vice-Presidential candidate, Lyndon Johnson invited him to spend a weekend at the LBJ ranch. During the visit, the President summoned him for a parley in the cow pasture, whereupon Humphrey promptly stepped in some cow dung.

"Mr. President," declared Hubert, regaining his equanimity and his balance, "I just stepped on the Republican platform!"

❧

Prime Minister Harold Macmillan recalls that when he was British Resident Minister in Algeria during World War II he was asked to settle a dispute between the British and American officers in the Allied mess. The Americans wanted drinks served before meals, the British after.

Macmillan's solution: "Henceforth, we will all drink before meals in deference to the Americans and we will all drink after in deference to the British."

🌿

Sir Winston Churchill, whose appreciation of liquor was well known, used to tell of the time he was scheduled to make a speech before a small gathering.

The chairman introduced him by saying: "If all the spirits consumed by Sir Winston were poured into this room, it would reach up to here on the wall."

He drew a line with his finger at about level with his eyes.

Churchill got up to speak. Glancing at the imaginary line on the wall, he looked up at the ceiling and made a mathematical calculation with his fingers. Then he sighed and said, "Ah, so much to be done, and so little time in which to do it."

Adlai Stevenson, commenting on the report that he really wanted the job of State Department consultant, used to tell the story of a drunk who called the hotel switchboard at 6 a.m. to ask when the bar would open.

"Nine a.m.," the telephone girl replied.

A half an hour later the man called again, asked the same question in thicker tones, and received the same response.

When, unmistakably drunk, he called again at 7, the girl said in exasperation, "For the third time, you can get in the bar at 9 a.m.!"

"Get in?" said the drunk, "I want to get out!"

❧

Llewellyn Thompson, the U.S. Ambassador to Russia, attended a dinner in Moscow at which former *Izvestia* editor Aleksei Adzhubei was also a guest. Suddenly Adzhubei's attention became fixed on a book of matches given to him by an American. He turned to Thompson saying, "Since we continually hear from your country that you are a peaceful people, what I see here astonishes me. I shall read it to you, Mr. Ambassador, and I ask you to tell me why such a peaceful nation prints such things on matchbooks." He looked around the room triumphantly before he read: "Enlist in the U.S. Army."

The room quieted as everyone watched Thompson examine the matchbook passed to him. Then he said with a smile, "I'm afraid that you are repeating a mistake too often made around here. You look only at one side of a story. If you will turn these matches over and read the other side, you will see that it says, 'Safety First. Prevent accidents.'"

John F. Kennedy once recalled, "Senator George Smathers has been one of my most valuable counselors at crucial moments. In 1952 when I was thinking of running for the United States Senate, I went to Senator Smathers and said, 'George, what do you think?' He said, 'Don't do it, can't win, bad year.' [That was the year Mr. Kennedy won his Senate seat.]

"In 1956 I didn't know whether I should run for Vice-President or not, so I said, 'George, what do you think?' And Senator Smathers replied, 'It's your choice!' So I ran and lost.

"In 1960 I was wondering whether I ought to run in the West Virginia primary, but the Senator said, 'Don't do it. That state you can't possibly carry.'

"And actually, the only time I really got nervous about the whole matter of Los Angeles was just before the balloting and George came up and said, 'I think it looks pretty good for you.'"

President Lyndon B. Johnson loves to tell about "the man who slept through the preacher's sermon down in my hill country. Every Sunday he would come and sit in the front row and sleep all during the sermon.

"Finally, the preacher got a little irritated, and one Sunday he said, 'All you people' — the fellow was snoring in the front row — and the preacher went on in a low voice, 'All you people who want to go to heaven, please rise.' Everybody stood up except the man who was asleep.

"When they sat down, the preacher said in a very loud voice that was calculated to arouse him, 'All of you men who want to go to hell, please stand up.' The man jumped up. He looked around in back of him, he looked at his wife, and she was sitting down. He looked at his grandmother, and she was sitting down, at his children, and they were sitting down. He looked at the preacher, somewhat frustrated, and he said, 'Preacher, I don't know what it is we are voting on, but you and I seem to be the only two for it.' "

❦

One of Barry Goldwater's favorites is the story about how "Khrushchev had certain problems. He found that Stalin's memory haunted him and finally he figured the best way to fix that was to get rid of Stalin's body. So he called President Kennedy and asked if he'd take the body. Kennedy explained he didn't want a Communist dead or alive in the United States, but suggested he call Macmillan.

"Macmillan gave Khrushchev the same line, that he would like to help him but it would cause too much political trouble, and suggested, 'Try de Gaulle. Every once in a while that fellow will help you, and besides he enjoys offending the Americans.'

"Well, de Gaulle explained to Khrushchev that he had trouble at home and abroad, but suggested he try Ben-Gurion: 'There's a little fellow who's pretty decent, and his country has the most relaxed immigration laws. He'll probably help you.'

"So Khrushchev called Ben-Gurion, told him his dilemma, and said, 'We'll bring the body in the dark of night, absolutely clandestinely, and you won't have anything to worry about.'

"Ben-Gurion answered: 'Oh, Mr. Khrushchev, don't give it a thought. We're tickled to death to help you. Just bring that body down here any time in broad daylight. We'll take care of it. But I have to remind you, Mr. Khrushchev, that my country has the highest rate of resurrection in the world.' "

❦

Arthur J. Goldberg, United States Ambassador to the United Nations, relates the story of an Iowa judge who was once called to San Francisco as a substitute for an ailing colleague. One of the first cases he was called upon to decide involved admiralty law. Being from Iowa, he had no specialized knowledge in admiralty law, so he asked the litigants if they wouldn't prefer that the case be postponed until the regular judge returned. The litigants said no, they would rather have him

decide it. Upon which the Iowa judge rejoined, "All right. But I want to make one thing clear. Let there be no moaning at the bar when I put out to sea."

※

Adlai Stevenson used to tell about the time he was interviewed by writers of a national TV show. One of them made a point of introducing himself and explaining: "I'll be sure to vote for you this election. I would have last time but I was sick on election day."

"Oh, that's what happened," Stevenson said, nodding. "I wondered."

Secretary of the Interior Stewart Udall tells of one incident during his visit with Nikita Khrushchev at the Black Sea. "He asked me if I wanted to have my picture taken with him, and I answered that I did. And just as the fellow was about to snap the picture he said, 'If it will help you out, you can go ahead and shake your finger in my face.'"

❦

Senator Robert Kennedy remembers how he once ran into difficulty in addressing the Foreign Student Council. Attempting to turn one of brother John's most famous phrases, Bob began,

"You people are exemplifying what my brother meant when he said in his inaugural address, Ask what you can do for — us — uh — do not ask what you can do — uh — ask, not what you can do for your country but — Well, anyhow, you remember his words!"

As the listeners laughed loudly, Bob added, "That's why my brother is President."

This was one of John F. Kennedy's favorites:

"Mr. Khrushchev himself, it is said, told the story a few years ago about the Russian who began to run through the Kremlin shouting, 'Khrushchev is a fool. Khrushchev is a fool.' He was sentenced, the Premier said, to twenty-three years in prison, 'three for insulting the Party Secretary, and twenty for revealing a state secret.' "

Adlai Stevenson often told a story he heard "from a schoolteacher in Chicago about a little Jewish boy who asked to be excused from school because it was Yom Kippur and his grandmother wanted him to be at home on that religious holiday. And the teacher excused him.

"On hearing that, a little Irish boy came up and asked to be excused too. The teacher said, 'But Patrick McCarthy, I know you are not Jewish.' He said, 'No, but I think grandmother is a little Jewish and I'm sure she wants me to be home with her.'

"Then, by golly, if a little colored boy didn't come up and ask if *he* couldn't be excused. She said to him, 'Well, now, Joseph, this is going too far. I know that you're not Jewish.'

"And he said, 'No, ma'am, I'm not, but I sure am in favor of this cause.'"

Former President Dwight Eisenhower recalls the conversation he once had with John Foster

Dulles during a short cruise in the Presidential yacht. They were discussing the anecdote about George Washington's ability to throw a silver dollar across the Potomac — from one shore to the other.

The yacht was passing the point where Washington was supposed to have performed his feat. Dulles remarked that the breadth of the river seemed so great that perhaps the story should be regarded as apocryphal.

"One thing must be remembered," said Eisenhower. "A dollar went a great deal further in those days than it does now."

President Johnson told a group of business leaders the following anecdote to explain why large funds were necessary for the missile race with the Russians:

"In 1861 a Texan left to join the rebels. He told his neighbors he'd return soon, that the fight would be easy, 'because we can lick those dam-yankees with broomsticks.'

"He returned two years later, minus a leg. His neighbors asked the tragic, bedraggled, wounded man what happened. 'You said it'd be easy, that

you could lick those damyankees with broom-sticks.'

" 'We could,' replied the rebel, 'but the trouble was the damyankees wouldn't fight with broom-sticks.' "

❦

Adlai Stevenson used to tell about a time he was being taxied to the airport and introduced himself and started chatting with the cabbie.

"People say I talk over the heads of the average man," Mr. Stevenson said. "What do you think?"

The cab driver deliberated, then answered, "Well, Governor, *I* understand you, but I'm not so sure about the average man."

❦

President Lyndon Johnson tells one story about "the Postmaster General who got a letter from a little boy who had lost his father, and whose widowed mother was having difficulty making ends meet. He wrote a letter to the Lord and said, 'Dear God, Please send Mom a hundred dollars to help with the family.'

"The letter wound up on the Postmaster General's desk and he was quite touched by it, so he took a twenty-dollar bill out of his pocket, put it in a Postmaster General's envelope, put an air-mail stamp on it, and sent it to the little boy.

"About two weeks later he got a letter back that said: 'Dear God, Much obliged for all you have done, but we need another hundred. And if you don't mind, when you send it to Mama, please don't route it through Washington, because they deducted eighty per cent of it last time.'"

❧

The subject of disarmament gave Winston Churchill occasion to tell this fable:

"Once upon a time, all the animals in the zoos decided that they would disarm, and they arranged to have a conference to arrange the matter. So the rhinoceros said, when he opened the proceedings, that the use of teeth was barbarous and horrible and ought to be strictly prohibited by general consent. Horns, which were mainly defensive weapons, would, of course, have to be allowed.

"The buffalo, the stag, the porcupine, and even the little hedgehog, all said they would vote

with the rhino. But the lion and tiger took a different view. They defended teeth, and even claws, which they described as honorable weapons of immortal antiquity. The panther, the leopard, the puma, and the whole tribe of small cats all supported the lion and the tiger.

"Then the bear spoke. He proposed that both teeth and horns should be banned and never used again for fighting by any animal. It would be quite enough if animals were allowed to give each other a good hug when they quarreled. No one could object to that. It was so fraternal and that would be a great step toward peace. However, all the other animals were very offended with the bear, and the turkey fell into a perfect panic.

"The discussion got hot and angry, and all those animals began thinking so much about horns and teeth and hugging when they argued about the peaceful intentions that had brought them together, that they began to look at one another in a very nasty way.

"Luckily, the keepers were able to calm them enough to go back quietly to their cages and they began to feel quite friendly toward one another again."

Senator Edward M. Kennedy was injured in a plane crash in June of 1964. Several days later while recuperating in a hospital, he was told by the doctor that he was doing quite well. Flat on his back, but still in full possession of his wit, Teddy replied, "That reminds me of a story. A prize fighter was taking a pasting from his opponent. When he returned to his corner at the end of the round, his manager told him he was doing great, that his rival had scarcely laid a glove on him. So the fighter told his manager to keep his eye on the referee then — 'Because someone in there is beating the daylights out of me.'"

Former President Truman likes to tell this story:

"In a Pennsylvania Dutch family, the old gentleman had been very ill, and on a restricted diet. One day the doctor told the family that the old man was going to die, and they might as well let him have anything he wanted to eat.

"So Mama, without of course repeating the doctor's grim prediction, went in to take Papa's order for supper. When the old man understood he could have anything he wanted, he asked for corned beef, fried potatoes, and half a gallon of coffee. 'And,' he concluded, 'you might be giving me a slice of that well-cured ham in the smoke-house.'

" 'Ah, Papa,' said his wife, 'the corned beef, the fried potatoes, and the coffee I am fixing yet, but the ham — ach, that we should save for the funeral.' "

When Konrad Adenauer, former West German Chancellor, was confined to bed with the grippe, he chaffed his doctor and said he had to recuperate because he was to make an official trip abroad.

"I'm not a magician," said the doctor. "I can't make you young again."

Adenauer responded: "I'm not asking that. I don't want to become young again; all I want is to go on getting old."

Former President Harry Truman recalls, "During one of my first sessions in the Senate, J. Hamilton Lewis came over and sat down by me.

He was from Illinois and was the whip in the Senate at that time. 'Don't start out with an inferiority complex,' he told me. 'For the first six months, you'll wonder how you got here — after that you'll wonder how the rest of us got here.' "

❦

Lynda Bird Johnson tells this anecdote about her mother, the First Lady:

"One day when Mother was shopping in a department store in Austin, she saw a lady who had worked very hard for years in my father's campaigns — she was a real party worker.

"Mother was in a great hurry and kept arguing with herself — should she take the time to go over and speak or should she just pretend she didn't see her? Of course, she finally went over and gave the lady a big hello. Well, the lady looked straight at Mother for a minute and then asked, 'Do I know you, dearie?' "

❦

· Vice-President Hubert Humphrey likes to tell the story of how, during the celebrated Cuban missile crisis of 1962, President Kennedy confided to him, "If I'd known the job was this tough, I wouldn't have trounced you in West Virginia."

Said Humphrey to the President, "If I hadn't known it was this tough, I never would have let you beat me."

❦

Former President Truman always enjoys telling this pointed anecdote:

"Once upon a time, there were a number of citizens who thought that Andrew Jackson ought to have a suitable coffin. At great expense, they went to Syria and purchased a marble sarcophagus. A sarcophagus, as you know, is a tomb — a big marble coffin with a marble lid. These citizens then shipped this box to Washington, which was quite a job, as it weighed four or five tons.

"At last, they thought, a suitable resting place had been provided for Andrew Jackson.

"Well, the only trouble with the project was that Andrew Jackson wasn't dead. Moreover, he wasn't ready to die. And he did not intend to be hurried to his grave.

"Courteously but firmly he wrote to these well-

meaning citizens and said, 'I must decline the intended honor.'

"And they never did get Old Hickory into that thing. You can still see it, if you're interested, out in front of the Smithsonian Institution. It still sits there. Andy wouldn't even be buried in it.

"I think that this little story has a moral in it. It is this: Before you offer to bury a good Democrat, you'd better be sure he is dead."

❧

John F. Kennedy liked to tell this story about the scramble for the 1960 Democratic Presidential nomination:

"Several nights ago I dreamed that the good Lord touched me on the shoulder and said, 'Don't worry, you'll be the Democratic Presidential nominee in 1960. What's more, you'll be elected.' I told Stu Symington about my dream. 'Funny thing,' said Stu, 'I had exactly the same dream about myself.'

"We both told our dreams to Lyndon Johnson, and Johnson said, 'That's funny. For the life of me, I can't remember tapping either of you two boys for the job.'"

Former President Eisenhower tells of one reunion with his four brothers at which a reporter asked the date of the previous reunion.

Ike remarked that they had all been together for his inauguration as president of Columbia University, but with little opportunity to talk. "The last real reunion," he said, "was in July 1946 at my fishing cabin in Wisconsin."

Brother Edgar interrupted in quick contradiction. The month, he said, was June, not July.

Ike retorted that he was prepared to lay ten dollars on the line to back his contention that it was July.

The reporter said, "General, you are sure you are right, are you?"

"No," Ike replied quickly, "but I'm sure Ed is always wrong."

❦

John F. Kennedy, speaking before the American Newspaper Publishers Association recalled "that in 1851, the *New York Herald Tribune*, under the sponsorship of Horace Greeley, employed as its London correspondent an obscure journalist by the name of Karl Marx.

"We are told that the foreign correspondent, Marx, stone-broke and with a family ill and undernourished, constantly appealed to Greeley and the managing editor Charles Dana for an increase in his munificent salary of $5 per installment, a salary which he and Engels labeled as the 'lousiest petty bourgeois cheating.'

"But when all his financial appeals were refused, Marx looked around for other means of livelihood and fame and eventually terminated his relationship with the *Tribune* and devoted his talents full-time to the cause that would bequeath to the world the seeds of Leninism, Stalinism, revolution, and the Cold War.

"If only this capitalistic New York newspaper had treated him more kindly, if only Marx had remained a foreign correspondent, history might have been different, and I hope all publishers will bear this lesson in mind the next time they receive a poverty-stricken appeal for a small increase in the expense account from an obscure newspaperman."

❧

Adlai Stevenson recalls the story of a man in his home town of Bloomington, Illinois, "who was interviewed by a newspaper reporter on his one-hundredth anniversary.

"After congratulating the old gentleman, the reporter asked a few questions. 'To what do you attribute your longevity?'

"The centenarian thought for a moment and holding up his hand and ticking off the items on his fingers, began: 'I never smoked, I never drank liquor, I never over-ate, and I always rise at six in the morning.'

"To that the reporter remarked: 'I had an uncle who acted the same way but he only lived to be eighty. How do you account for that?'

" 'He didn't keep it up long enough,' came the reply."

It is always a source of considerable consternation for a public official to be introduced in laudatory terms which no one could live up to. At moments like these, Arkansas Senator J. William Fulbright frequently lightens things up with this tale: "A farmer was leading a cantankerous calf across a bridge. Halfway across, the calf froze and refused to budge. A car pulled up behind and the farmer, explaining the problem to the motorist, asked him to honk his horn. Maybe, he suggested, the noise might scare the calf into motion.

"The driver obliged. The horn blared and the calf, terrified, leaped into the air, plunged over the bridge rail, and drowned.

"The farmer, infuriated, turned to the motorist and upbraided him viciously for killing the calf.

" 'But you asked me to honk,' the driver protested.

" 'Sure,' said the farmer, 'but you didn't have to honk so big for such a little calf.' "

❧

Clare Boothe Luce, former U.S. ambassador to Italy, tells about a big reception at which the hand-shaking line suddenly stopped, leaving a flustered American girl standing in front of the ambassador. "Oh, Mrs. Luce," she said, "it's so wonderful to be over here in Rome seeing all these old romantic ruins — and you, too!"

❧

Massachusetts Senator Edward Kennedy recalls one memorable early political experience:

"I ran for the Senate at a very young age, and one of the issues used by the opposition was that I had never worked a day in my life.

"One day I was going through one of the factories in my state to meet the workers. And I will never forget the fellow who came up to me, shook my hand, and said: 'Mr. Kennedy, I understand you never worked a day in your life. Let me tell you, you haven't missed a thing.' "

❧

Former President Dwight Eisenhower tells of an air raid while he was visiting the British sector of the front. The British general rushed over to be sure the Supreme Commander was unhurt. General Eisenhower thanked him for such solicitude for his safety.

"Oh," the candid Briton replied, "my concern was that nothing should happen to you in *my* sector."

❧

When Queen Elizabeth and Prince Philip came to this country in 1957 they visited a supermarket. As they walked down an aisle together a woman hurried up to the Prince. "Aren't you supposed to be walking two steps behind the Queen?" she asked.

"You're quite correct, Madam," Philip replied. "But I think it's all right. You see, yesterday we sat together at a football game and we became quite chummy."

❧

Robert F. Kennedy tells how teamster boss Jimmy Hoffa, with whom he had more than a passing acquaintance, attempted to rally his powerful union against the Kennedy family, and was joined by several other union leaders. When the notorious Brooklyn gangster Joey Gallo asked if his influence might be of some help in the campaign, Bobby replied, "Just tell everybody you're voting for Nixon."

❧

Australia's former Prime Minister Robert Menzies recalls that when he first succeeded to his party's leadership he was needled by a hostile reporter who asked, "I suppose you will consult the powerful interests who control you before you choose your Cabinet?"

Replied Menzies, "Naturally, but please, young man, keep my wife's name out of this."

🏵

Adlai Stevenson relates "a story my grandfather Stevenson, a devout Presbyterian, told about the preacher who was driving along a back road in the South when he espied a parishioner wearily clearing up a poor, stony field.

" 'That's a fine job you and the Lord have done clearing up that rocky field,' he shouted.

" 'Thank you, parson,' the man replied, 'but I wish you could have seen it when the Lord had it all to himself.' "

🏵

Ethel Kennedy, wife of Robert F. Kennedy, tells how she once gave a dinner for thirty in honor of the Dowager Duchess of Devonshire. The dinner guests were jammed elbow to elbow in the small dining room, when Ethel bowed her head to say her customary grace. But she startled them by adding: "And, please, dear God, make Bobby buy me a bigger dining room table."

Former Senator from New York Kenneth Keating tells about a candidate for the House of Representatives who was orating with great verbal vigor before a street-corner gathering during the critical pre-election period.

One voter who had listened to every word shouted up to the candidate when he had finished his speech, "I wouldn't vote for you if you were Saint Peter himself!"

To which the candidate replied, "My friend, if I were Saint Peter, there's no possible way you could vote for me. You wouldn't be in my district!"

❦

Mayor John Lindsay of New York tells about a factory owner with one hundred forty-eight employees who proposed a profit-sharing and pension plan — provided every employee signified his approval in writing. One hundred forty-seven men signed immediately, but one refused, thereby balking the entire project. For two weeks the holdout persisted, then one day he marched into the boss's office and declared meekly, "I've decided to sign."

"Good," said the boss, "but what finally persuaded you to change your mind?"

Explained the maverick: "This morning the two huskiest members of the union grabbed me by the collar and said to me, 'If you haven't signed up by ten-thirty this morning, we'll break both your arms, break both your legs, and knock out all your teeth.' Well, boss, nobody had ever bothered to explain the plan to me so clearly before."

❦

Michigan's Governor George Romney tells about the guest of honor at a banquet who discovered at the last moment that his upper plate had cracked. "You'll have to cancel my speech," he told the toastmaster.

"Nonsense," said the toastmaster. "Here's a spare upper I have in my pocket."

The guest of honor put the denture in his mouth, and attempted a few words with poor results. "No good," he announced, removing the plate. "It doesn't fit."

The toastmaster quickly produced a second plate, which didn't fit either, and then a third plate, which fit perfectly.

The guest of honor made a fine speech, received an ovation, then turned gratefully to the toastmaster. "It was a lucky break for me," he said, "that you happen to be a dentist."

"Dentist nothing," said the toastmaster. "I'm an undertaker."

General Dwight D. Eisenhower tells the story of the time he was heading the Allied forces in Europe near the end of World War II. He and a member of his staff were on an inspection tour when they were caught in a sudden downpour. The two generals managed to find a couple of tarpaulins to throw over their shoulders, but their feet were soaked.

They sighted a supply depot where General Eisenhower asked a corporal, "Could we have some fresh boots?"

"Sure," said the corporal. "How big's your feet?"

"Nine-and-a-half," answered Ike.

"You'll take eights," said the corporal.

General Eisenhower was struggling to get the small boots on his wet feet, when the tarpaulin slipped off his shoulders and revealed the cluster of five stars on each one.

"Holy Moses!" gasped the corporal. "It's the Milky Way!"

⚜

One of Lyndon Johnson's many anecdotes is about "that judge down in Texas during the depression when they called him up one night, a state senator did, and said, 'Judge, we just abolished your court.'

"The Judge said, 'Why did you abolish my court?'

"And the state senator replied, 'Well, we have

to consolidate the courts for economy reasons. Yours was the last one created.'

"And the judge said, 'You didn't do it without a hearing, did you? Who would testify that my court ought to be abolished?'

"The state senator said, 'The head of the bar association.'

"The judge said, 'Let me tell you about the head of the bar association. He is a shyster lawyer and his daddy ahead of him was.'

"Then the state senator said, 'The mayor of the city came down and testified.'

"And the judge said, 'Let me tell you about that mayor. He stole his way into office. He padded the ballot boxes. He counted them twice. Who else testified?'

"The state senator said, 'The banker.'

"And the judge said, 'He has been charging usury rates like his daddy and his granddaddy ahead of him.'

"The state senator said, 'Judge, I don't think we should talk any more tonight. Your blood pressure is going up. The legislature did adjourn. Somebody did offer an amendment to abolish your court. I was kidding. No one testified against you at all. But I have fought the amendment and

killed it. I thought it would make you feel better.'

"The judge said, 'I know, but why did you
make me say those things about three of the
dearest friends I ever had?'"

❈

Harry Truman tells about the time a visitor
called on his mother a few weeks after he had
been inaugurated as President. "My, but you
must be proud of your boy Harry," gushed the
visitor. "Of course I am," said Mrs. Truman,
"but I've got another son just as fine — right out
there in that field — plowing."

❈

One of President Eisenhower's favorite golfing
stories concerns one fellow who was being asked
to complete a foursome by three of his golfing
friends.

"I'm sorry, but I don't think my wife would
like it," replied the hesitant golfer.

"Aw, come on," importuned one of the friends,
"are you a man or a mouse?"

"Oh, I'm a man, all right," he replied. "My
wife is afraid of a mouse."

J. Edgar Hoover relates this story of a con man who thought he knew all the angles. After laboring tirelessly to perfect the signature of a society bigwig, the swindler successfully passed off a forged check to a local merchant. Inspired by his first success, he returned to cash a second check, only to be arrested. The first check had been returned with the notation, "Insufficient Funds."

In August, 1964, during the tense days before President Johnson announced his choice of a running mate for Vice-President, Hubert Humphrey patiently waited for Johnson's decision. Three days before the deadline for decision, Humphrey, on his way to a reception, was stopped in a hotel lobby by a local television interviewer.

Nervously waving a microphone in his face, the interviewer asked quickly, "Senator, do you know anything? Are you nervous? Are you anxious? How are you bearing up?"

"Obviously, a lot better than you are," Humphrey replied calmly.

Senator Robert Kennedy recalls that during his 1962 visit to Japan at a Buddhist Temple in Osaka a priest gave him a stick of incense to burn. Kennedy asked Ambassador Reischauer if such a gesture were permissible, and Reischauer indicated that it was merely a demonstration of respect.

"You're sure it won't look as if I'm worshiping Buddha?" asked the Roman Catholic Kennedy. Reischauer again assured him that it was all right. Kennedy picked up the incense, still muttering, "If I get kicked out —"

❧

One of Senator Everett Dirksen's favorite stories is the one about the two deacons, a Republican and a Democrat, kneeling together in church.

"The Republican deacon," relates Dirksen, "was praying to the Lord and saying: 'O, Lord make us Republicans unlike the Democrats; make us hang together in accord, make us hang together in concord.' And just then his Democratic brother said, 'Lord, any cord will do.' "

Defense Secretary Robert S. McNamara tells of a departmental aide who overheard another aide talking to himself.

"Let's face it," said the first. "You're nuts."

"But talking to myself doesn't make me crazy," countered the other.

"No, that doesn't — but you *listen!*"

An aide was giving General Charles de Gaulle the final results of his overwhelming victory in the 1962 national election and concluded, "*Mon Dieu!* You've done better than ever."

"True," answered de Gaulle nonchalantly. "But please, just call me '*mon général.*'"

J. Edgar Hoover loves to tell about the time when there was a hunt on for a dangerous criminal. The F.B.I. sent to all police chiefs throughout the country four photos of the wanted man: a front, back, left profile, and right profile. In a few hours Hoover got a telegram from a rural police chief, reading: "I got your photographs and have caught all four men."

❦

When Soviet Premier Khrushchev made his entry into New York's Plaza Hotel, many residents, including some elderly and well-dressed women, were standing in the lobby. They booed him loudly. Khrushchev turned abruptly as he was about to enter the elevator. He looked back at the women and said, "Boo!" and he entered the elevator.

❦

Senator Robert F. Kennedy tells of the time he wanted to phone Senator Edward V. Long (Dem.-Mo.). By mistake he reached Senator Russell B. Long (Dem.-La.), who corrected him.

"Ah," said Bobby politely, "this is the good Long?"

"This is Russell Long," replied the Senator, unwilling to agree he was the good Long. Then he asked: "Now, which Kennedy is this?"

❦

Vice-President Hubert Humphrey likes to tell freshmen Congressmen how one junior member of his family reacted to the move to Washington after his first election to the Senate in 1948. The night before the Humphreys left Minneapolis, the new Senator overheard his young daughter's bedtime prayers. After asking God to bless her father and mother and the rest of the family, she added, "And now, good-bye, God. We're going to Washington."

❦

Secretary of Labor W. Willard Wirtz tells about receiving a letter from an eleven-year-old girl saying that she had been elected "labor secretary" of her fourth-grade class.

Her duties, Wirtz reports, consisted of "cleaning the blackboard and putting the chalk back. On Fridays I have to clean up the room and take care of anything that is in the wrong place. Please write and tell me what *your* duties are."

Wirtz's reply was simply, "Same here."

❦

John F. Kennedy delighted in telling this story about the time he "was up in New York, stressing physical fitness, and in line with that, Arthur Goldberg went to Switzerland with a group to climb some of the mountains. They got up about five and he was still in bed. He joined them later, but when they all came back at four o'clock in the afternoon he didn't come back with them.

"So they sent out search parties and there was not a sign that afternoon and night. The next day the Red Cross went out and around calling: 'Goldberg, Goldberg! It's the Red Cross!' Then this voice came down from the mountain: 'I gave at the office!' "

❦

Vice-President Hubert Humphrey likes to tell this story on himself:

After one of his speeches, a woman dragged her five-year-old son up to the Veep, telling the lad, "I want you to meet Mr. Humphrey."

"I already know him," the boy protested. "I see him every night on the Humphrey-Brinkley Show!"

❧

Prince Bernhard of the Netherlands told this story about a British lady who wondered what kind of wedding gift to get for Crown Princess Beatrix. "After all," she said, "you just don't go out and buy an electric toaster for a Crown Princess."

Prince Bernhard told her that he would ask the royal couple for their preference. Bernhard asked his daughter, then reported to the lady, "They'd like an electric toaster."

♦ ♦ ♦ THE WILD WORLD OF SPORTS

Leo Durocher recalls coaching at first base in an exhibition game the Giants were playing at West Point. One raucous cadet sitting in the stands was trying his best to rile "the Lip."

"Hey, Durocher!" the cadet yelled. "How did a little squirt like you get into the major leagues?"

"My Congressman appointed me," retorted Leo.

●

Michigan State's football coach Duffy Daugherty recalls the time he received a letter addressed to "Duffy the Dope."

"Didn't that make you mad?" someone asked.

"I didn't mind getting the note," answered Daugherty. "It was pretty funny. The thing that bothered me was that the East Lansing post office knew exactly where to deliver it."

●

Joe DiMaggio tells how a baseball player discovers that his youth is going. "You start chasing a ball and your brain immediately sends out commands to your body — 'Run forward!' 'Bend!' 'Scoop up the ball!' 'Peg it to the infield!' "

"Then what happens?" asked a friend.

"Then," said Joe, "your body says, 'Who, me?' "

●

Jackie Robinson, the first Negro to play major-league baseball, entered the big leagues with a wry, subdued sense of humor. He likes to recall how on the day of his first appearance, he kissed his wife good-bye at their hotel and said, "Honey, if you come out to Ebbets Field today you won't have any trouble recognizing me." He paused and then added, "My number is 42."

●

Joe McCarthy, former manager of the New York Yankees, tells about the time he dreamed that he had died and gone to heaven. There he was ordered by St. Peter to assemble and manage a baseball team. McCarthy says his eyes glistened as he surveyed the talent around him — Christy Matthewson, Walter Johnson, Rube Waddell, Babe Ruth, Lou Gehrig, and scores of other baseball greats. "This will be the greatest team of all time," he said proudly. Just then the phone rang. It was Satan calling from below to challenge the heavenly nine to a ball game.

"But you haven't a chance of winning!" McCarthy told him. "I've got all the best baseball players."

"Oh, I know," Satan replied. "But I've got all the umpires."

•

The great Bobby Jones loved to tell about "the veteran caddies at St. Andrews, Scotland. They are in a group to themselves in experience, dignity, wisdom. One, in particular, a veteran perhaps seventy years old, was carrying the clubs of an unpleasant duffer who played very poor golf and who blamed everything on the caddy.

"Throughout the ordeal the old caddy maintained a dignified silence. But finally when the duffer, addressing the other members of his foursome, remarked: 'I believe on this round I've drawn the worst caddy in the world,' the veteran quietly interposed: 'Oh, no, sir. That would be too great a coincidence.'"

•

Cassius Clay remembers the time an unknown

puncher knocked him off his feet for a couple of moments during a bout in Madison Square Garden:

"Every now and then I gotta get hit to realize I'm like other people," conceded Cassius graciously.

Yogi Berra loves to retell the story of how the Yankees' manager Casey Stengel tried to break him of the habit of swinging at bad balls. "Study the pitcher," Stengel advised. "Study every throw carefully."

Berra listened carefully, nodded, then went up and swung and missed at three perfect strikes.

"Whaddaya expect me to do?" Yogi grumbled as he returned to the bench. "Swing and think at the same time?"

•

Gil Hodges tells of how he once turned down a steak dinner on an airplane because it was Friday. A teammate, also a Catholic, advised him to have the steak, explaining: "There's an automatic dispensation when you're on a plane and they're serving only meat."

Hodges still refused. "That might be, but we're a little too close to headquarters up here," he said.

•

Joe Garagiola grew up with Yogi Berra in St. Louis, and loves to recount stories like this one about the ex-Yankee great:

"Yogi is the kind of guy who will make a remark you won't pay much attention to at the time. But then it will come back to haunt you. I remember a bunch of us were discussing the way

103

attendance was falling off in Kansas City. Everybody offered a theory, and then Yogi said, 'Well if people don't come out to the ball park, who's going to stop them?' You know? It sounds almost right, but it will start keeping you awake nights later. You'll find yourself walking the floor and asking yourself, 'What did he say, what did he say?' "

●

Stan Musial relates the story about a fellow who was driving to a mountain resort. A policeman stopped him and said, "Did you know you're riding without tail lights?" The driver got out of the car noticeably shaken by this piece of information. The officer tried to reassure him. "It's not too much of an infraction," he said. "Nothing to get upset about."

"It may not mean much to you," the driver replied. "But to me it means I've lost a trailer, a wife, and four kids!"

●

Byron Nelson remembers the time he suggested that Danny Kaye enter a golf tournament for pro-amateur twosomes. Kaye replied that he'd be too self-conscious. Nelson replied that surely five hundred people couldn't make Kaye nervous. "As an entertainer," Kaye answered, "I have appeared before fifty thousand people without being nervous. But there I knew what I was doing."

Some time later Kaye was appearing at a theatre. In the audience were Nelson and other top golf pros. Kaye introduced them, brought them on stage, and invited them to sing. They all froze. "See?" Kaye said to Nelson. "Now you're on my golf course."

●

The New York Yankees' star outfielder, Joe Di-Maggio, hit successfully in fifty-six consecutive games. His string was almost broken some games earlier when his own brother Dom, playing for the Boston Red Sox, robbed him of a sure hit with a fantastic catch against the center-field wall. Di-Mag got his hit on his next and last time at bat, but still was muttering over brother Dom's catch when he came back to the clubhouse. "This speaks well for the integrity of the game," he remarked, "but the kid sure didn't have to rub it in that way — especially when he's coming to my house for dinner tonight!"

•

Baseball's Jimmy Piersall tells of the time Charles O. Finley, owner of the Kansas City team, issued free tickets to Catholic high school students for a Friday night game. "He let in 7,500 people and won't sell a single hot dog," cracked Piersall.

•

A notorious bad ball hitter, Yogi Berra tells of the time he went fishing for a terrible pitch and struck out. A deep silence greeted him on his return to the dugout. Yogi waited futilely for a word from someone, but the silence endured. Finally the irrepressible catcher exclaimed, "How can a pitcher that wild stay in the league!"

•

Knute Rockne, the famed Notre Dame football coach, used to tell of a time he was deeply disappointed at the showing made by his team in the first half of an important game.

At half-time the chagrined teammates hud-
dled together, awaiting a 10-minute tongue-lash-
ing from their coach. But Rockne failed to show
up. Finally, at the last possible moment he
strolled in and remarked casually, "All right, girls,
it's time for the second half."

Notre Dame won by three touchdowns.

•

Dizzy Dean once promised a hospital full of
crippled kids that he would strike out the playing manager of the New York Giants, Bill Terry.
The kids assured Dizzy they would be listening
to the radio, and the braggadocio Diz said he
would, if possible, fan Terry with the bases full.
Well, in the ninth inning of the game the next day
— with two out, and the Cards a run to the good
— the first two men hit safely. Critz was the next
batter, and Dean purposely passed him to get to
Terry. As the Giant manager strolled to the plate,
Diz walked over and smiled, "Gee, Bill, I hate
to do this, but I promised some kids I'd fan you
with the bases full. That's why I walked Critz."

Then the Dizzy one went back to the rubber
and poured two fast strikes across the plate. Instead of wasting the next one, Diz wound up

and threw it waist-high across the plate for strike three, and Terry just stared at it. Dizzy came to the bench laughing to himself: "Bill never figured I'd dare groove that last one!"

•

Mickey Mantle, never much for after-dinner speaking engagements, recalls one such dreaded affair in St. Petersburg, Florida, at which master of ceremonies Larry McQueen announced there would be no speeches.

Then in the next breath he called upon Mantle to say a few words.

Mickey instantly replied, "When Mr. McQueen said there would be no speeches, I tore mine up."

•

Henry Aaron tells that during a World Series against the Yankees, he stepped to the plate. Yogi Berra told him, "You've got the trademark in the wrong place. It should be in the front." Hank replied, "I get paid for hitting, not reading."

♦ ♦ ♦ BELLES LETTRES, BEAUX ARTS, AND BELLY LAUGHS

Frank Lloyd Wright told of the time during a trial that he was called to the witness stand and sworn under oath. He wore his white hair long, and was elegantly dressed in the style of a nineteenth-century Westerner. The county attorney began the examination. "Your name?"

"Frank Lloyd Wright."

"Your occupation?"

Wright sat up straighter, adjusted the silk handkerchief in his suit pocket, and rapped his cane on the floor for emphasis.

"I'm the world's greatest living architect."

An exasperated friend later asked Wright how he could say such a thing.

"I had to," Wright answered. "I was under oath."

Carl Sandburg recalls that he once was persuaded to attend the dress rehearsal of a very serious play by a very serious young dramatist. Unfortunately, Sandburg slept through most of the performance. The outraged young playwright berated him later, "How could you sleep when you knew how much I wanted your opinion?"

"Young man," Sandburg countered, "sleep *is* my opinion."

Playwright Jean Cocteau tells this story:

"A few years ago, after having presented toys to all my grandnephews and grandnieces, I suddenly remembered that I had a godson whose existence I always forgot. Well, I wanted to redeem myself. I went to a big shop, I selected the biggest teddy bear they had — one with big blue eyes — and I sent it out to the poor little forsaken one.

"I found out later that for five years he had been a colonel, fighting in Indo-China."

✿

Harry Hershfield loves to tell this tale:

"France wanted to buy the Rock of Gibraltar. They approached England and the English said: 'No dice, the Rock of Gibraltar is the image of British greatness. Anyway, if we did sell it to you, you couldn't give it a suitable name.' 'Oh yes we can,' replied the French, 'we'd call it de Gaulle Stone.'"

✿

The illustrious painter Picasso was entertaining some friends at lunch in his house in the south of France. One of them looked around and said, "I notice you don't have any Picassos on your walls, Pablo — why is that? Don't you like them?"

"On the contrary," Picasso answered, "I like them very much. It's just that I can't afford them."

Albert Einstein used to tell of the time he was asked by his hostess at a social gathering to explain the theory of relativity. Said the great scientist, "Madam, I was once walking in the country on a hot day with a blind friend, and said that I would like a drink of milk.

"'Milk?' said my friend, 'Drink I know; but what is milk?'

"'A white liquid,' I replied.

"'Liquid I know; but what is white?'

"'The color of a swan's feathers.'

"'Feathers I know; what is a swan?'

"'A bird with a crooked neck.'

"'Neck I know; but what is this crooked?'

"Thereupon I lost patience. I seized his arm and straightened it. 'That's straight,' I said; and then I bent it at the elbow. 'That's crooked.'

"'Ah!' said the blind man, 'now I know what you mean by milk!' "

Louis Untermeyer, the poet and anthologist, recalls telling a Texas audience all his best stories. After the lecture he was presented with his check, which he then realized had been rather a financial burden on the committee. With a flourish of his hand, he generously offered it back, to be put to some good use. The committee hesitated. They then retired to decide what to do. The problem settled, they returned, accepted the check, and explained that it would be used to start a special fund.

"And the purpose of this fund?" asked Mr. Untermeyer.

"It's a fund to get better lecturers next year," they answered sadly.

❦

Pablo Picasso tells of the time an American businessman, who always wanted to own a real "Picasso," obtained permission to visit the great artist's studio. Endeavoring to flatter the painter into a generous gesture, the visitor praised everything. Finally he saw a simple line drawing, half-buried in a waste-basket. Removing it reverently, he inquired, "How much is this?"

"As a token of friendship," Picasso replied, "take it for $35,000."

❦

The late architect Frank Lloyd Wright used to tell how one rainy night he was awakened from a sound sleep by an urgent phone call from a client who had just moved into his Wright-designed house.

"There's a leak in the roof and the living room is flooded," cried the man. "What shall I do?"

Advised Wright, "Rise above it."

۞

Pablo Picasso relates the story of an American GI who met him in Paris and told Picasso that he didn't like modern paintings because they weren't realistic. The artist made no immediate reply. A few minutes later the soldier showed him a snapshot of his girl friend.

"My word," exclaimed Picasso, "is she *really* as small as all that?"

S. J. Perelman tells of an encounter aboard a train. A loquacious conductor told him that he had been riding in trains for so long that he had begun to smell like one. "Sure enough," adds Perelman, "two brakemen waved their lanterns at him a short time later and tried to tempt him down a siding in Kansas City. It came as a blow when I heard the next morning that he had fallen off the train during the night. The fireman said that we had circled about for an hour trying to find him but that it had been impossible to lower a boat because we did not carry a boat."

❧

Artur Rubinstein remembers that once, in order to practice for a concert, he told his butler, François, to tell any callers that he was not at home. When the telephone rang, a woman asked for the maestro. With the thunderous chords of Rubinstein's rehearsal echoing from the next room, the butler casually told the woman that his master was out. "Out?" she protested. "But I can hear him playing!"

"Not at all, madam," the quick-witted butler informed her. "It is merely I, dusting the keys."

Washington humorist Art Buchwald likes to tell "the story of the hard-luck guy who had nothing but trouble. Finally, he jumped out of an airplane with two parachutes — neither one worked. As he fell through the air, he yelled 'St. Francis, St. Francis, help me!' and a hand reached out of the clouds; grabbed him by the collar and held him safe in midair.

"Then a deep voice from the sky spoke and asked, 'Were you calling St. Francis of Assisi or St. Francis Xavier?' The man screamed: 'Xavier!' The voice said, 'Sorry' as the hand opened and let him drop."

The late poet Robert Frost, long time "Poet in Residence" at Amherst, used to tell about a remarkable answer given by one of his students to a question on the final examination. Frost, always reluctant to give his students written exams, had asked, simply, "What good did my course do you?"

His favorite student's reply was equally brief: "Not a dam bit."

"I gave that lad a ninety," recalled Frost, "and I would have made it a hundred if he hadn't left the 'n' off 'damn!' "

Pablo Picasso says that once a girl reporter asked him why mature men generally look younger than mature women. Picasso thought for a minute, then explained, "It's because a woman of forty is usually fifty."

❦

Igor Stravinsky relates the story of how he was once offered $4,000 to compose the music for a Hollywood film. "It is not enough," he said.

"It's what we paid your predecessor," replied the producer.

"My predecessor had talent," answered Stravinsky. "I have not. So for me, the work is more difficult."

❦

Eugene Ormandy relates the story of how he once held an audition at Carnegie Hall for a singer to perform for him with the Philadelphia Orchestra. Joanna Simon, the beautiful five-foot-ten opera singer, stepped onto the stage to begin her audition. Ormandy looked at the young beauty and gasped; "Now that you have the job, what're you going to sing?"

Artur Rubinstein recounts the story of how he stood in the lobby before one of his sell-out concerts and watched the crowd go in. The box-office attendant noticed him loitering and said, "I'm sorry, mister, but I can't seat you."

"Then," replied Rubinstein, "may I be seated at the piano?"

❀

Carl Van Doren relates: "In my youth on the farm I was preparing one fall to attend a nearby carnival. A hired man suggested feminine companionship.

" 'Why'n't you ask one o' the gals hereabouts t' go with y'?' he inquired.

119

"I replied that I was awkward and unschooled in the art of persuading females. 'I wouldn't know,' I confessed, 'how to ask 'em.'

"It was then that the sage philosopher gave me counsel I have ever remembered:

" 'Heck, bub,' he said, 'there ain't no *wrong* way!' "

✿

Pianist Artur Rubinstein is fond of telling this story on himself:

Some months ago he was assailed by a stubborn case of hoarseness. The newspapers were full of reports about smoking and cancer; so he decided to consult a throat specialist. "I searched his face for a clue during the thirty-minute examination," Rubinstein says, "but it was expressionless. He told me to come back the next day. I went home full of fears and I didn't sleep that night."

The next day there was another long examination and again an ominous silence.

"Tell me," the pianist exclaimed. "I can stand the truth. I've lived a full, rich life. What's wrong with me?"

The physician said, "You talk too much."

♦ ♦ ♦ ♦ ♦ A FUNNY
THING HAPPENED
ON THE WAY TO THE PULPIT

Cardinal Spellman remembers watching a World Series baseball game when the Dodgers still played in Brooklyn. A high foul fly was hit over his box seat. Roy Campanella, the Dodger catcher attempted to catch it but missed, and the ball caromed against the Cardinal's knee. Campy asked anxiously if he had been injured.

"Don't worry about it, Roy," the Cardinal said. "A priest's knees are the toughest and the most thickly padded part of his anatomy."

Cardinal Richard J. Cushing recalls the 1948 Fourth of July celebration in Boston, where he was scheduled as final speaker at the Hatch Memorial Shell on the Charles River. A quarter of a mile away at historic Boston Common a huge fireworks display was set to conclude the festivities.

Unfortunately, the timing was off, and the then Archbishop Cushing stepped on the stage ten minutes past his scheduled time. He had just begun with "ladies and gentlemen" when the sky erupted with multicolored pyrotechnics, followed by deafening explosions of miniature bombs.

Patiently the Archbishop stood in the center of the stage until the last bomb echoed off in the distance. Then, clearing his throat, he continued, ". . . and in conclusion . . ."

✠

Billy Graham recalls that during his New York City crusade, the evangelist asked former Congressman Brooks Hays to say a brief greeting at the opening of one of his meetings. Hays replied that Graham was being unscriptural.

"What do you mean?" Graham asked.

"Well," said Hays, "the Bible says, 'Thou shalt not muzzle the ox that treadeth out the corn.'"

✠

Bishop James A. Pike recalls an incident while he was speaking at the University of California at Berkeley, when someone brought up the sub-

ject of San Francisco's notorious "topless danc-
ers."

Intoned Pike: "We must always be in a posi-
tion of thanksgiving to God for the beauties of
his handiwork."

✛

"I heard about one man," tells Billy Graham,
"who happened to remember his wife's birthday,
and he rushed to the drugstore and got candy and
flowers. He had never done it before. He went
home and rang the doorbell, and he was singing
'Happy Birthday, dear sweetheart,' and she
came to the door and burst into tears.

"She said, 'Oh Jim, this has been a terrible day;
the children have been bad, the roast burned,
the phone has rung all day, and now you come
home drunk.' "

✛

Pope John XXIII, always conscious of his family's humble origins, told this story after someone
suggested that he confer titles of nobility on his
brothers:

One day, during the Pope's nunciature in Paris,
his brothers, Alfredo and Severo, purchased black
suits to wear to a solemn official ceremony. Nei-

ther of them knew how to knot his tie, and in despair they had turned to him for assistance. The Nuncio, also incapable of accomplishing the task, summoned his secretary who also turned out to be incompetent. Finally it was the Nuncio's chauffeur who managed to complete the job of dressing his brothers in their formal attire.

☩

This is one of Billy Graham's favorites:

"I heard about a man who was about to be electrocuted for murder and it was his morning to go. There were about eight other men on death row. As he walked silently toward the electric chair one of his fellow inmates said, 'God bless you, Joe,' another one said, 'Good luck, Joe,' and when he came to the last man everybody had said everything he could think of to say, so he said, 'More power to you, Joe.'"

☩

Bishop Fulton J. Sheen registered at a Minneapolis hotel and filled out a guest card at the desk. After the word "Representing" he wrote: "Good Lord and Company."

Norman Vincent Peale recalls that he was once invited to speak in a church out West that he had never visited previously. The chairman of the group sponsoring him advised him, "Be sure to speak up good and loud this evening, Dr. Peale. The agnostics here are something awful."

✢

Evangelist Billy Graham likes to tell the story of the lady who said to her minister, "This morning I stood in front of the mirror for half an hour admiring my beauty. Do you think I committed the sin of pride?" The minister replied, "No, I don't think you committed the sin of pride — it was more the sin of faulty imagination."

✢

Francis Cardinal Spellman frequently spends his Christmas overseas with our Armed Forces. On one trip a colonel was showing Cardinal Spellman the maps and photographs of some recent action when an interoffice speaker switched on. A voice came through, saying, "There's a little fellow in a clergyman's collar coming over to see you. Give him the two-dollar show."

The colonel coolly notified the voice that the Cardinal was already there, and the speaker quickly clicked off. Trying to dismiss the incident, the colonel showed Cardinal Spellman the works. When the tour was over, Spellman thanked the colonel and added, "I thought that show was worth at least three dollars."

✝

After addressing a group of teachers and nuns at the College of St. Francis in Joliet, Illinois, Bishop Fulton J. Sheen asked for written questions from the floor. The nuns gasped when Bishop Sheen read one of the questions: "Would you please use your influence with the Mother Superior to allow the nuns to watch you on television?" But they applauded when the Bishop pleaded: "Mother Superiors everywhere, please let your nuns see my program." Then he added, "I am just a humble instrument. The good Lord rode into Jerusalem on an ass and He can go into television on one."

✝

Evangelist Billy Graham tells one story about his crusade in Scotland, where he received his

greatest acclaim. He was staying at an Edinburgh hotel and one morning at breakfast he was delighted to hear the strains of "Onward Christian Soldiers" coming from the cook in the kitchen. He tiptoed to the door and said a few words to her by way of felicitation.

"Oh," said the Scot, "I always sing that hymn when I boil eggs. Three verses for soft, and five for hard-boiled."

✝

Bishop Fulton J. Sheen relates that an outspoken astronomer once told him, "To an astronomer, man is nothing but an infinitesimal dot in an infinite universe."

"An interesting point of view," returned the Bishop, "but you seem to forget that your infinitesimal dot of a man is still the astronomer."

If you liked the illustrations in this book by NCS award-winner Al Kilgore...

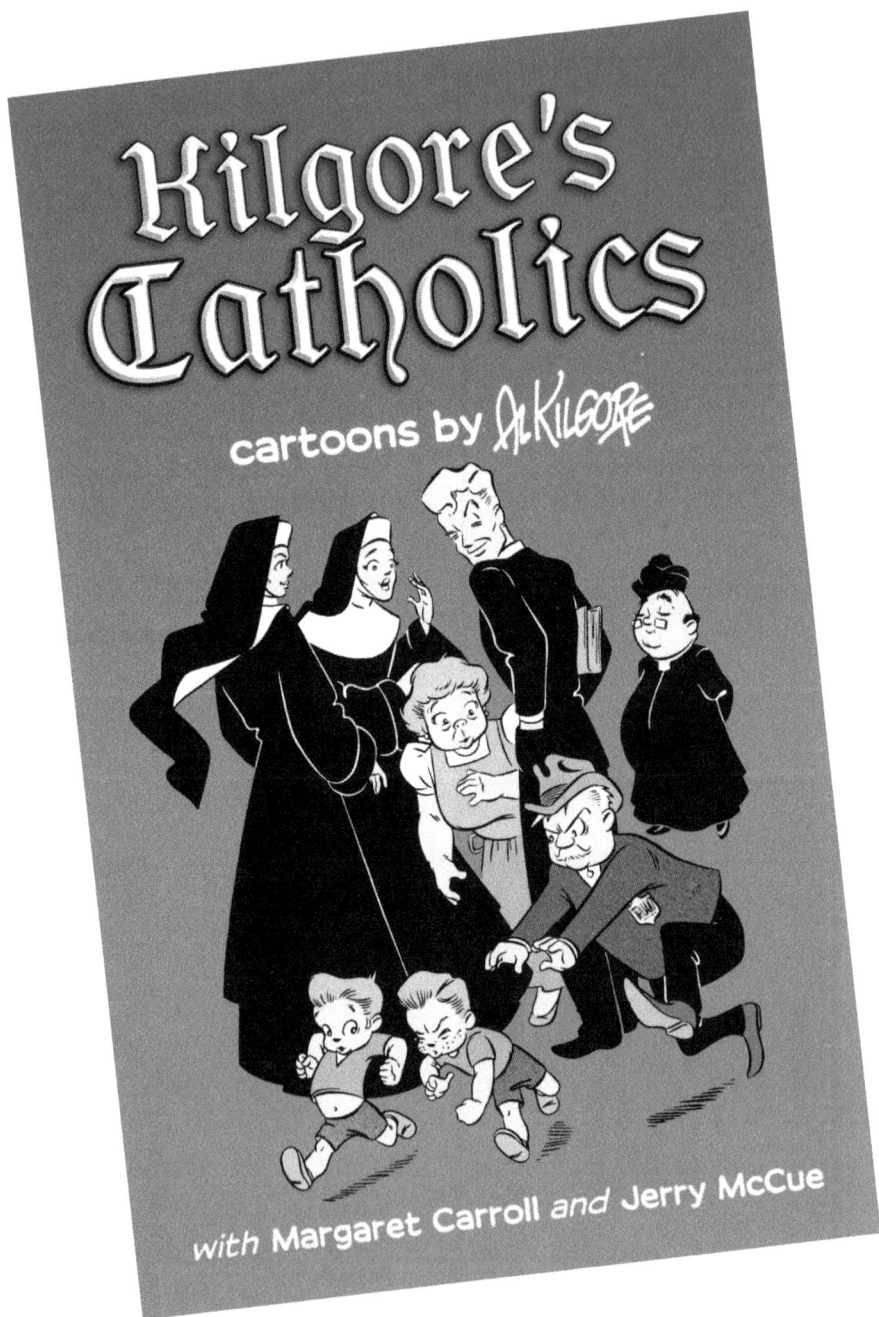

...then About Comics has some books for you!

Little Gabriel

Al Kilgore

www.ingramcontent.com/pod-product-compliance
Lightning Source LLC
Chambersburg PA
CBHW060807050426

42449CB00008B/1584